BRITISH LIBRARY DIARY 2019

FRANCES
LINCOLN

COVER Details from: A map of the world showing the voyages of Captain James Cook, from *Tallis's Illustrated Atlas, and Modern History of the World, Geographical, Political, Commercial, and Statistical*, published in London by John Tallis and Co., 1851; Detail of a map of the Southern Hemisphere showing the route of the *Resolution* during Captain James Cook's second voyage, from Cape Town in November 1772 to Caledonia in October 1774

PREVIOUS PAGE A portable terrestrial globe, by John Betts, produced in London by George Philip & Son, c.1890

British Library Pocket Diary 2019
© 2018 Quarto Publishing plc
Images and text © 2018 The British Library
Astronomical information © Crown Copyright. Reproduced by permission of the Controller of Her Majesty's Stationery Office and the UK Hydrographic Office (www.ukho.gov.uk)

First published in 2018 by Frances Lincoln, an imprint of the Quarto Group
The Old Brewery, 6 Blundell Street, London N7 9BH, United Kingdom
www.QuartoKnows.com

Every effort is made to ensure calendrical data is correct at the time of going to press but the publisher cannot accept any liability for any errors or changes.

A catalogue record for this book is available from the British Library

ISBN 978-0-7112-3955-5

Printed and bound in China

9 8 7 6 5 4 3 2 1

2019

JANUARY
M	T	W	T	F	S	S
	1	2	3	4	5	6
7	8	9	10	11	12	13
14	15	16	17	18	19	20
21	22	23	24	25	26	27
28	29	30	31			

FEBRUARY
M	T	W	T	F	S	S
				1	2	3
4	5	6	7	8	9	10
11	12	13	14	15	16	17
18	19	20	21	22	23	24
25	26	27	28			

MARCH
M	T	W	T	F	S	S
				1	2	3
4	5	6	7	8	9	10
11	12	13	14	15	16	17
18	19	20	21	22	23	24
25	26	27	28	29	30	31

APRIL
M	T	W	T	F	S	S
1	2	3	4	5	6	7
8	9	10	11	12	13	14
15	16	17	18	19	20	21
22	23	24	25	26	27	28
29	30					

MAY
M	T	W	T	F	S	S
		1	2	3	4	5
6	7	8	9	10	11	12
13	14	15	16	17	18	19
20	21	22	23	24	25	26
27	28	29	30	31		

JUNE
M	T	W	T	F	S	S
					1	2
3	4	5	6	7	8	9
10	11	12	13	14	15	16
17	18	19	20	21	22	23
24	25	26	27	28	29	30

JULY
M	T	W	T	F	S	S
1	2	3	4	5	6	7
8	9	10	11	12	13	14
15	16	17	18	19	20	21
22	23	24	25	26	27	28
29	30	31				

AUGUST
M	T	W	T	F	S	S
			1	2	3	4
5	6	7	8	9	10	11
12	13	14	15	16	17	18
19	20	21	22	23	24	25
26	27	28	29	30	31	

SEPTEMBER
M	T	W	T	F	S	S
						1
2	3	4	5	6	7	8
9	10	11	12	13	14	15
16	17	18	19	20	21	22
23	24	25	26	27	28	29
30						

OCTOBER
M	T	W	T	F	S	S
	1	2	3	4	5	6
7	8	9	10	11	12	13
14	15	16	17	18	19	20
21	22	23	24	25	26	27
28	29	30	31			

NOVEMBER
M	T	W	T	F	S	S
				1	2	3
4	5	6	7	8	9	10
11	12	13	14	15	16	17
18	19	20	21	22	23	24
25	26	27	28	29	30	

DECEMBER
M	T	W	T	F	S	S
						1
2	3	4	5	6	7	8
9	10	11	12	13	14	15
16	17	18	19	20	21	22
23	24	25	26	27	28	29
30	31					

2020

JANUARY
M	T	W	T	F	S	S
	1	2	3	4	5	
6	7	8	9	10	11	12
13	14	15	16	17	18	19
20	21	22	23	24	25	26
27	28	29	30	31		

FEBRUARY
M	T	W	T	F	S	S
					1	2
3	4	5	6	7	8	9
10	11	12	13	14	15	16
17	18	19	20	21	22	23
24	25	26	27	28	29	

MARCH
M	T	W	T	F	S	S
						1
2	3	4	5	6	7	8
9	10	11	12	13	14	15
16	17	18	19	20	21	22
23	24	25	26	27	28	29
30	31					

APRIL
M	T	W	T	F	S	S
		1	2	3	4	5
6	7	8	9	10	11	12
13	14	15	16	17	18	19
20	21	22	23	24	25	26
27	28	29	30			

MAY
M	T	W	T	F	S	S
				1	2	3
4	5	6	7	8	9	10
11	12	13	14	15	16	17
18	19	20	21	22	23	24
25	26	27	28	29	30	31

JUNE
M	T	W	T	F	S	S
1	2	3	4	5	6	7
8	9	10	11	12	13	14
15	16	17	18	19	20	21
22	23	24	25	26	27	28
29	30					

JULY
M	T	W	T	F	S	S
		1	2	3	4	5
6	7	8	9	10	11	12
13	14	15	16	17	18	19
20	21	22	23	24	25	26
27	28	29	30	31		

AUGUST
M	T	W	T	F	S	S
					1	2
3	4	5	6	7	8	9
10	11	12	13	14	15	16
17	18	19	20	21	22	23
24	25	26	27	28	29	30
31						

SEPTEMBER
M	T	W	T	F	S	S
	1	2	3	4	5	6
7	8	9	10	11	12	13
14	15	16	17	18	19	20
21	22	23	24	25	26	27
28	29	30				

OCTOBER
M	T	W	T	F	S	S
			1	2	3	4
5	6	7	8	9	10	11
12	13	14	15	16	17	18
19	20	21	22	23	24	25
26	27	28	29	30	31	

NOVEMBER
M	T	W	T	F	S	S
						1
2	3	4	5	6	7	8
9	10	11	12	13	14	15
16	17	18	19	20	21	22
23	24	25	26	27	28	29
30						

DECEMBER
M	T	W	T	F	S	S
	1	2	3	4	5	6
7	8	9	10	11	12	13
14	15	16	17	18	19	20
21	22	23	24	25	26	27
28	29	30	31			

INTRODUCTION

The British Library Diary for 2019 is illustrated with maps from one of the world's largest historical collections, with a chronological spread of over 2,000 years. The British Library has 4.5 million maps, plans and views from across the world, ranging from Medieval times to the present day, and with its many atlases, topographical views, globes, hand-drawn and printed maps, models and digital data, this collection can justifiably claim to be the greatest.

The maps which appear within the pages of this diary show a variety of different places and have been drawn in different styles, from a dissected globe to a map of the moon, from the voyages of Captain James Cook to the Chinese New Year. The depth of the collection can be seen in the different views of cartographers and publishers across many centuries. Some of the maps show scenes of human endeavour and activity, while others show buildings and animals. These maps had important meaning to the period in which they were made, but there is also a more playful side, with maps used as games. Whichever period they are from, maps are some of the world's most significant historical items and we hope you enjoy the rich and diverse range included here.

Philips' Handy Volume Atlas of the British Empire, by J.F. Williams, produced in London and Liverpool by George Philip & Son, 1887

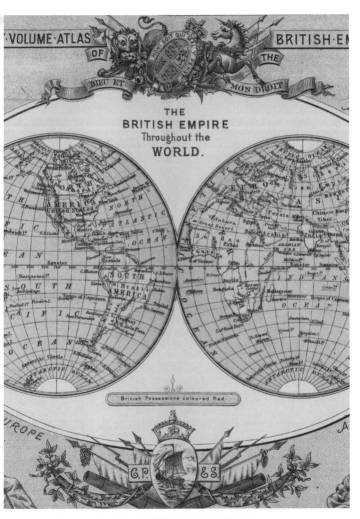

VOLUME·ATLAS OF THE BRITISH·EMPIRE

THE
BRITISH EMPIRE
Throughout the
WORLD.

British Possessions coloured Red.

DECEMBER · JANUARY

31 Monday   New Year's Eve

---

01 Tuesday   New Year's Day
                              Holiday, UK, Republic of Ireland, USA, Canada,
                                        Australia and New Zealand

---

02 Wednesday   Holiday, Scotland and New Zealand

---

03 Thursday

---

04 Friday

---

05 Saturday

---

06 Sunday   *New Moon*
                                                   Epiphany

A comprehensive Chinese map delineating heaven and earth, the myriad countries
of the world and ancient and modern human affairs

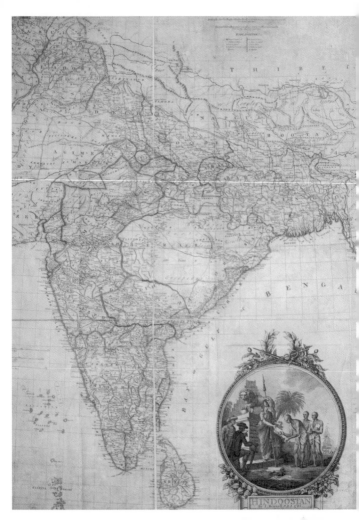

JANUARY

Monday 07

Tuesday 08

Wednesday 09

Thursday 10

Friday 11

Saturday 12

Sunday 13

Hindoostan, a map by J. Rennell from 1782, engraved by J. Phillips and produced in
London by W. Faden, 1785

JANUARY

14 Monday

First quarter

15 Tuesday

16 Wednesday

17 Thursday

18 Friday

19 Saturday

20 Sunday

Detail from a map of Japan by Ishikawa Ryusen, 1687

伊豫

土佐一郡

八万石
松平大和

八万石
松平大和

稲葉石見

今パリ

三万石余
松平左京

十五万石
松平隠岐

松山

四万石
松平讃河

一万石
松平若京

大町
カナメ
クルミ
ニシ

五万石余
加茂左江

大洲

伊達遠江

七万石

吉高

伊豫喜内

三万石
山内大善

糸川

大川関

長濱

不二川

ニリ

ホド
サカ関

ホド

セリ

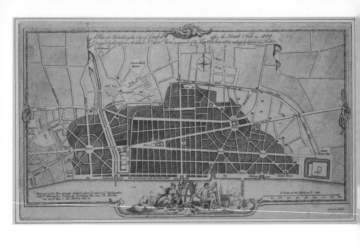

Notes

JANUARY

Monday 21

Full moon
Holiday, USA (Martin Luther King Jnr Day)

Tuesday 22

Wednesday 23

Thursday 24

Friday 25

Australia Day

Saturday 26

Last quarter

Sunday 27

A Plan for Rebuilding the City of London after the Great Fire in 1666,
by Sir Christopher Wren, c.1800

JANUARY · FEBRUARY

28 Monday

Holiday, Australia (Australia Day)

---

29 Tuesday

---

30 Wednesday

---

31 Thursday

---

01 Friday

---

02 Saturday

---

03 Sunday

A Chart of Part of the North Coast of New Zeland; the Bay of Plenty, from
Cape Runaway to Cape Colvill, drawn on board the HMS *Endeavour* during
Captain James Cook's first voyage, 1771

A CHART OF PART OF THE NORTH COAST OF NEW ZELAND

FEBRUARY

04 Monday   *New moon*

05 Tuesday   Chinese New Year

06 Wednesday   Accession of Queen Elizabeth II
Holiday, New Zealand (Waitangi Day)

07 Thursday

08 Friday

09 Saturday

10 Sunday

Philips' Planisphere, showing the principal stars visible for every hour in the year, 1887

Notes

FEBRUARY

11 Monday

12 Tuesday   *First quarter*

13 Wednesday

14 Thursday   *Valentine's Day*

15 Friday

16 Saturday

17 Sunday

Map for a game, 'The Silver Bullet or The Road to Berlin', the aim of which is to manoeuvre a ball along a hollowed-out track to reach Berlin, produced in London by R. Farmer & Son, 1914

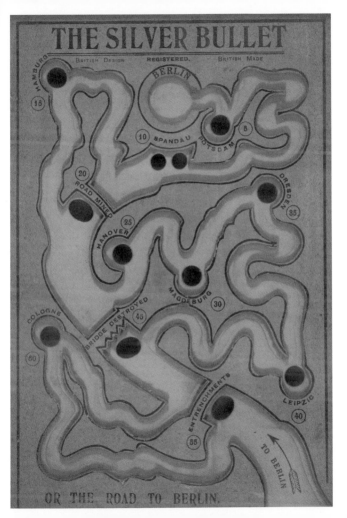

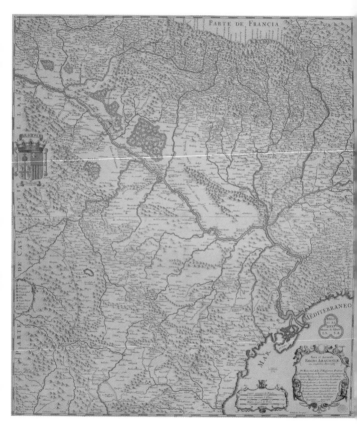

PARTE DE FRANCIA

MEDITERRANEO

MAR

FEBRUARY

Holiday, USA (Presidents' Day)

Monday 18

Full moon

Tuesday 19

Wednesday 20

Thursday 21

Friday 22

Saturday 23

Sunday 24

A map of the kingdom of Aragon, which includes administrative subdivisions by provinces, cities, towns, archbishoprics, bishoprics, monasteries, sanctuaries, rivers and mountain ranges, by J. Seyra et Ferrer, Zaragoza, 1715

FEBRUARY · MARCH

25 Monday

26 Tuesday   *Last quarter*

27 Wednesday

28 Thursday

01 Friday   St David's Day

02 Saturday

03 Sunday

A map of Belgium and surrounding area, depicted as a lion, by N.J. Piscatore, 1656

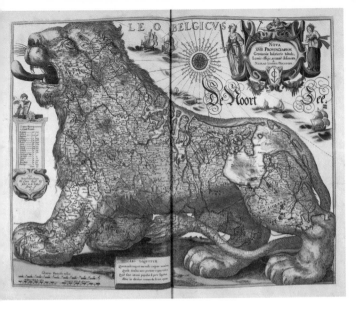

l'aÿde de nos
tir seigneur
nous divons

anaens nont point diuise
equalement Car asie vient
de midi par orient iusques

MARCH

Monday 04

Shrove Tuesday

Tuesday 05

New moon
Ash Wednesday

Wednesday 06

Thursday 07

Friday 08

Saturday 09

Sunday 10

Detail of a miniature of a map of the world divided into three parts; Europe, Asia and Africa, from Jean Corbechon's French translation of *De proprietatibus rerum* by Bartholomaeus Anglicus, printed in Lyons, 1482

MARCH

11 Monday
Commonwealth Day

12 Tuesday

13 Wednesday

14 Thursday
First quarter

15 Friday

16 Saturday

17 Sunday
St Patrick's Day

A map of Ireland made in 1610 by John Speed, and sold by John Sudbury & George Humble, London, 1614

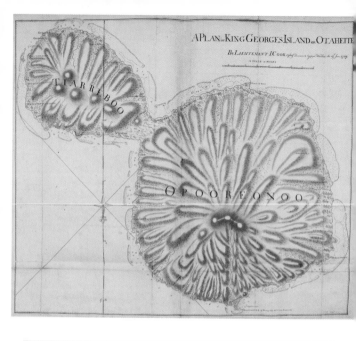

A PLAN of KING GEORGES ISLAND or OTAHEITE

By LIEUTENANT J COOK 1769 Drawn to Part Nautica the 13 of Jun 1769

A SCALE of MILES

TIARREBOO

OPOOREONOO

Notes

MARCH

Holiday, Northern Ireland and Republic of Ireland
(St Patrick's Day)

Monday 18

Tuesday 19

Vernal Equinox (Spring begins)

Wednesday 20

Full moon

Thursday 21

Friday 22

Saturday 23

Sunday 24

A Plan of King George's Island, or Otaheite, drawn on board the HMS *Endeavour* during
Captain James Cook's first voyage, 1769

MARCH

25 Monday

26 Tuesday

27 Wednesday

28 Thursday   *Last quarter*

29 Friday

30 Saturday

31 Sunday   Mothering Sunday, UK and Republic of Ireland
                                                            British Summer Time begins

Eastern Turkey, compiled at the Intelligence Division, War Office,
by Major F.R. Maunsell etc., London, 1901–1917

LAKE VAN

VAN GEUL

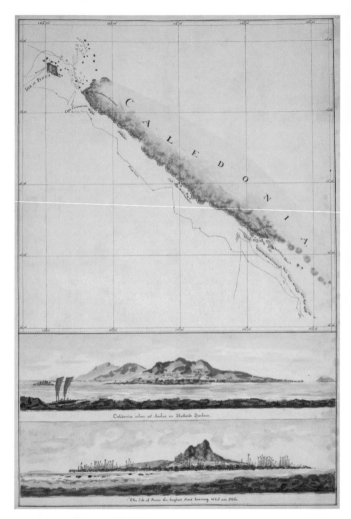

Caledonia when at Anchor in Bulladie Harbour.

The Isle of Pines the highest Part bearing W.S.S. one Mile.

APRIL

Monday 01

Tuesday 02

Wednesday 03

Thursday 04

New moon   Friday 05

Saturday 06

Sunday 07

Map of New Caledonia, with two coastal views; Ballarde Harbour and the Isle of Pines,
from Captain James Cook's second voyage, 1774

APRIL

08 Monday

09 Tuesday

10 Wednesday

11 Thursday

12 Friday											*First quarter*

13 Saturday

14 Sunday											Palm Sunday

Le Clerogéographie, a board game based on the geography of France,
with eighty-six lithographed maps, each on a card, France, c.1855

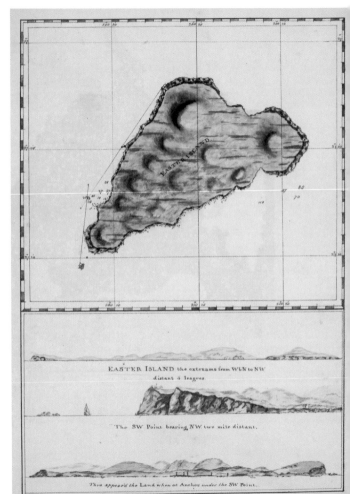

EASTER ISLAND the extreams from WbN to NW
distant 4 leagues

The SW Point bearing NW two mile distant.

Thus appear'd the Land when at Anchor under the SW Point.

APRIL

Monday 15

Tuesday 16

Wednesday 17

Maundy Thursday   Thursday 18

Full moon   Friday 19
Good Friday
Holiday, UK, Canada, Australia and New Zealand

First day of Passover (Pesach)   Saturday 20

Easter Sunday   Sunday 21
Birthday of Queen Elizabeth II

Chart and drawings of Easter Island, from a collection of sixty-seven charts
and maps illustrating the voyages and surveys of Captain James Cook and
other discoverers, c.1760–1780

APRIL

---

22 Monday

Easter Monday
Holiday, UK (exc. Scotland), Republic of Ireland,
Australia and New Zealand

---

23 Tuesday

St George's Day

---

24 Wednesday

---

25 Thursday

Holiday, Australia and New Zealand (Anzac Day)

---

26 Friday

Last quarter

---

27 Saturday

---

28 Sunday

A map of the city of Vicenza by Giandomenico Dall'Acqua, 1711

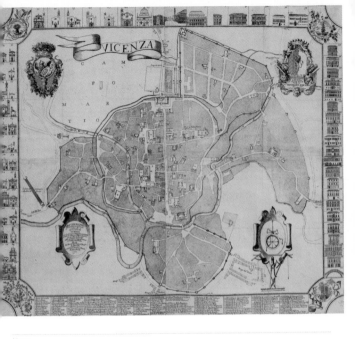

Notes

APRIL · MAY

Monday 29

Tuesday 30

Wednesday 01

Thursday 02

Friday 03

New moon   Saturday 04

Sunday 05

Detail of a map of the Caspian Sea by Johann Homann, Nuremburg, c.1720

MAY

06 Monday

Early Spring Bank Holiday, UK
Holiday, Republic of Ireland
First day of Ramadan (subject to sighting of the moon)

07 Tuesday

08 Wednesday

09 Thursday

10 Friday

11 Saturday

12 Sunday

First quarter
Mother's Day, USA, Canada, Australia
and New Zealand

A physical and political map in twelve segments to form a globe, produced
in Brussels by Merzbach & Falk, 1881

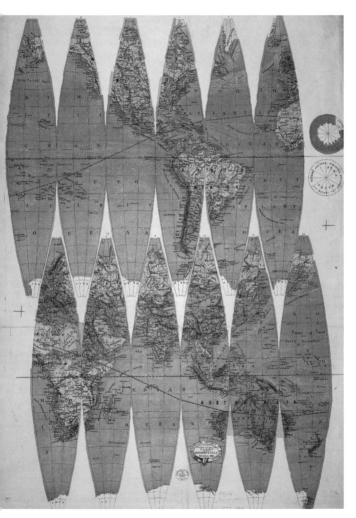

MAY

Monday 13

Tuesday 14

Wednesday 15

Thursday 16

Friday 17

Full moon

Saturday 18

Sunday 19

Woodcut illustration for *Utopia* by Sir Thomas More, 1518

MAY

20 Monday   Holiday, Canada (Victoria Day)

21 Tuesday

22 Wednesday

23 Thursday

24 Friday

25 Saturday

26 Sunday   *Last quarter*

Map of the course of the River Severn from Gloucester to Cardiff, produced in England
in the late 16th century

Notes

MAY · JUNE

Spring Bank Holiday, UK
Holiday, USA (Memorial Day)

Monday 27

Tuesday 28

Wednesday 29

Ascension Day

Thursday 30

Friday 31

Saturday 01

Coronation Day

Sunday 02

Portolan chart of western Europe and the Mediterranean, with the principal powers indicated by means of flags, by Pietro Vesconte, from a book of maps to accompany *Liber secretorum fidelium crucis*, originally produced in Venice, c.1320–1325

JUNE

03 Monday

New moon
Holiday, Republic of Ireland
Holiday, New Zealand (The Queen's Birthday)

04 Tuesday

05 Wednesday

Eid al-Fitr (end of Ramadan)
(subject to sighting of the moon)

06 Thursday

07 Friday

08 Saturday

The Queen's Official Birthday
(subject to confirmation)

09 Sunday

Whit Sunday
Feast of Weeks (Shavuot)

Detail of a map of the Island of Kiushiu, produced in Nagasaki, 1813

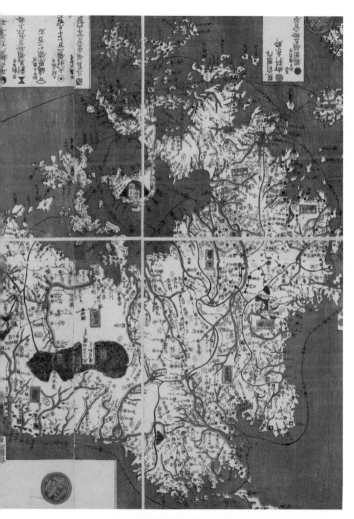

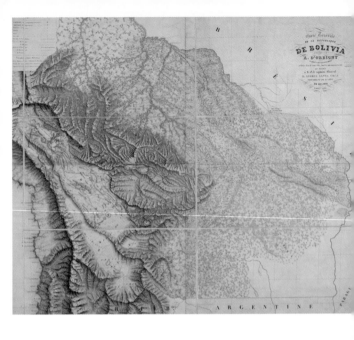

Notes

JUNE

First quarter
Holiday, Australia (The Queen's Birthday)

Monday 10

Tuesday 11

Wednesday 12

Thursday 13

Friday 14

Saturday 15

Trinity Sunday
Father's Day, UK, Republic of Ireland,
USA and Canada

Sunday 16

A map of the Republic of Bolivia by Charles d'Orbigny, Paris, 1839

JUNE

17 Monday   *Full moon*

18 Tuesday

19 Wednesday

20 Thursday   Corpus Christi

21 Friday   Summer Solstice (Summer begins)

22 Saturday

23 Sunday

A Description of the Passage of the Shadow of the Moon over England, In the Total
Eclipse of the Sun, on the 22nd Day of April 1715, in the Morning, by Edmund Halley

A Description of the Passage of the Shadow of the Moon, over England, In the Total Eclipse of the SUN, on the 22 Day of April 1715 in the Morning.

THE GERMAN SEA

SCOTLAND

THE IRISH SEA

IRELAND

St GEORGES CHANNEL

THE CHANNEL

FRANCE

I. Wight

A Scale of 60 computed Miles

Engrav'd by John Senex

The late Eclipse having not for many Ages been seen in the Southern Parts of Great Britain, I thought it not improper to give the Publick an account thereof, that the sudden darkness wherein the Stars will be visible about the Sun, may give no surprize to the People, who would, if unadvertised, be apt to look upon it as Ominous, and to Interpret it as portending evil to our Sovereign Lord, King George, and his Government, which GOD preserve. Hereby they will see that there is nothing in it more than Natural, and no more than the necessary result of the Motions of the Sun and Moon; And how well those are understood will appear by this Eclipse.

According to what has been seriously Observed, compared with our best Tables, we conclude the Center of the Moon's shade will be very near Lizard point, where about 9 min. past Eight at London, and that from thence in Eleven minutes of time, it will traverse the whole Kingdom, passing by Plymouth, Bristol, Glocester, Daventry, Peterborough, to Boston, near where it will leave Island. On both sides of this tract it will still decline, being so less and less in time, as you are nearer those limits, which are represented in the Scheme, passing on the one side near Chester, Leeds, and York, and on the other by Chichester, Gravesend, and Harwich.

At London we compute the Middle to fall at 13 min. past 9 in the Morning, when by darkness whether it will be a Total Eclipse or no. At London being so near the Southern Limit, the Beginning will be there at 7 min. past Eight, and End at 22 min. past Nine. The Oval figure shows & spans & Shadow will take up at time of the Middle at London, and its Center will pass over & Equinoctial, with a Velocity of nearly 30 Geographical Miles in a min. of time.

N.B. that (serious as these & Observe it, and especially the Appearance of Total darkness, with all the care they can,) for shortly the situation and Durations of the Shadow will be nicely determined, and by means thereof we may be enabled to Predict the like Appearances for future, to a greater degree of certainty than can be pretended to at present; for want of such Observations.

By their humble Servant Edmund Halley

JUNE

Monday 24

Last quarter

Tuesday 25

Wednesday 26

Thursday 27

Friday 28

Saturday 29

Sunday 30

Detail of a map of Sicily, from a Maritime Atlas of the World, signed Jouannes Olius, 1638

JULY

01 Monday
Holiday, Canada (Canada Day)

02 Tuesday
New moon

03 Wednesday

04 Thursday
Holiday, USA (Independence Day)

05 Friday

06 Saturday

07 Sunday

The Empire State, a map of New York with a plan of Central Park, published
in New York by Ensign, Bridgman & Fanning, c.1862

Notes

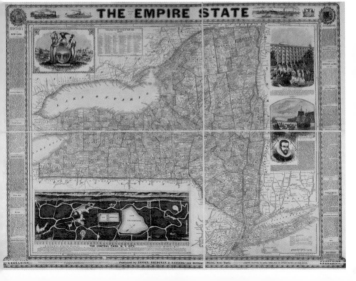

E U R O P E

A S I E

A R A B I E

SAHARA OU GRAND DÉSERT

DÉSERT DE

Tropique du Cancer

Tropique du Capricorne

O C É A N   A T L A N T I Q U E

M E R   A U S T R A L E

CARTE
DE L'AFRIQUE
dressée et dessinée
SOUS LA DIRECTION
de
Mʳ. J. G. Barbié du Bocage

ÉCHELLE (30,000,000)

JULY

Monday 08

First quarter

Tuesday 09

Wednesday 10

Thursday 11

Holiday, Northern Ireland (Battle of the Boyne)

Friday 12

Saturday 13

Sunday 14

A map of Africa, produced under direction of Mr J.G. Barbié du Bocage and
published in Paris, c.1875

JULY

15 Monday   St Swithin's Day

16 Tuesday   *Full moon*

17 Wednesday

18 Thursday

19 Friday

20 Saturday

21 Sunday

A General Map of the World, on the spherical projection, produced
in London by Richarde Jhones, 1576

Notes

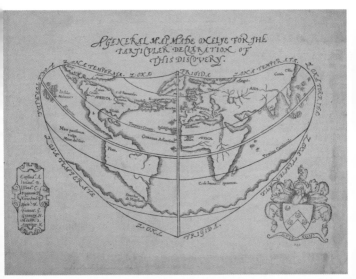

Wallis's
New GAME of
WANDERERS
in the
WILDERNESS

Monday 22

Tuesday 23

Wednesday 24

Last quarter

Thursday 25

Friday 26

Saturday 27

Sunday 28

A map of South America from Wallis's New Game of Wanderers in the Wilderness,
produced in London by Edward Wallis, c.1844

JULY · AUGUST

29 Monday

30 Tuesday

31 Wednesday

01 Thursday *New moon*

02 Friday

03 Saturday

04 Sunday

A map of Robert Louis Stevenson's *Treasure Island* by Walter Paget,
published in London by Cassell & Co., 1899

Treasure Island

AUGUST

Holiday, Scotland and Republic of Ireland

Monday 05

Tuesday 06

First quarter

Wednesday 07

Thursday 08

Friday 09

Saturday 10

Sunday 11

Detail of A Zoological Map of the World, Shewing the Geographical Distribution of Animals, published in London by W. Spencer, 1845

AUGUST

12 Monday

13 Tuesday

14 Wednesday

15 Thursday   *Full moon*

16 Friday

17 Saturday

18 Sunday

A map of Asia in the form of a jigsaw puzzle, from a set of four continents believed to be the first purpose-made jigsaw puzzles, produced in London by John Spilsbury, 1767

Notes

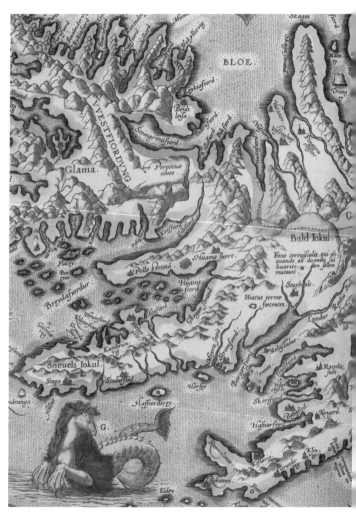

Skagin

BLOE.

Maln ey

Drang

WESTFIORDVNG

Rykiafiord

Beidi leisa

Steingrimsfiord

Glama.

Perpetuæ nives

Varanes

Trowbay

Dygra elofter

Kroffiord

Gilsfiord

Myrar

Bald Iokul

Flacey

Huams suert

Fons cereuisialis, qui ali-
quando ob dominiiis
auariti: iam folitos
mutauit.

Pella strand

Hiatus terræ
fœtentes

Staphfole.

Huams fiord

Breydafiortur

Hrunsfiord

Altafiord

Skogar strand

Salgyrn snoie

Stromsfiord

Lundur

Borger fiord

Melafandur

Hualfiord

Mofpelz snie

Sneuels Iokul.

Kumbrum vig

Stapa

Stadarfied.

Hrsfey

Vder eloster

Skeriford

Kongard

Befofiod

Hafnarfiord

Haffiorderey

G

drangæ

Ramalnes

Reglauig

Grunda

Klin vig

Eldry

Reyknues

AUGUST

Monday 19

Tuesday 20

Wednesday 21

Thursday 22

Last quarter   Friday 23

Saturday 24

Sunday 25

Detail of a map of Iceland by Abraham Ortelius, Antwerp, 1598

AUGUST · SEPTEMBER

---

26 Monday   Summer Bank Holiday, UK (exc. Scotland)

---

27 Tuesday

---

28 Wednesday

---

29 Thursday

---

30 Friday   *New moon*

---

31 Saturday

---

01 Sunday   Islamic New Year
                                        Father's Day, Australia and New Zealand

---

A map of the northern part of the Ottoman Empire by Giovanni Antonio Rizzi Zannoni, 1774

Notes

Godolfin

Lesfion as Cunrch tower

the ougab
wthere ys besẽt
wth londõ

manor de Senet

Loo

the mownt a lege
le to newlyn a myle
on newlyn de

SEPTEMBER

Holiday, USA (Labor Day)
Holiday, Canada (Labour Day)

Monday 02

Tuesday 03

Wednesday 04

Thursday 05

First quarter

Friday 06

Saturday 07

Sunday 08

Detail showing the bay of Penzance from a coloured chart, or bird's eye view, of the southern coast of England from Land's End to Exmouth, drawn c.1539

SEPTEMBER

09 Monday

10 Tuesday

11 Wednesday

12 Thursday

13 Friday

14 Saturday   *Full moon*

15 Sunday

Detail from A Complete Map of Japan, with its principal land and sea routes, Osaka, 1775

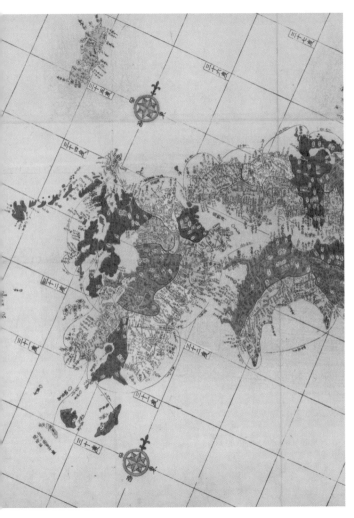

Stratton
Downdock
Bascestle
Titragill
Trewena
Padstow
Camelford
Launston
Colombe
Bruard
Badman
S Cler
S Ive
Lesthiell
Liskerd
S Ann's
Thuro
Grampont
W Low
Yokns
Aufill
Gwithis
S Ithes
Redruth
Pensans
Market Iew
Penry
Burien
Helston
Tregnye
Atonye
Foye
Dudman P
Mounts Bay
S Michael Mont
Pende
ys
Cury
S
Falmouth Haven
Ses ard P
The Manacles
Grude
Rame Head

5 10

Length. ——————————— 65.
Bredth. ——————————— 30.
Circumference. ——————— 262.
Launstō. { D. from Lon. 170. 216.
{ Latitude. 50. 42.

SEPTEMBER

Monday 16

Tuesday 17

Wednesday 18

Thursday 19

Friday 20

Saturday 21

Last quarter

Sunday 22

A map of Cornwall from a pack of cards representing the fifty-two counties of England
and Wales, produced in London by R. Morden, W. Berry, R. Green & G. Minikin, 1676

SEPTEMBER

23 Monday   Autumnal Equinox (Autumn begins)

24 Tuesday

25 Wednesday

26 Thursday

27 Friday

28 Saturday   *New moon*

29 Sunday   Michaelmas Day

Detail from a map of the Kingdom of Naples, by Giovanni Antonio Rizzi Zannoni,
Naples, 1788–1812

G O L F O

D I N A P O L I

I. DI CAPRI

G O L.

Notes

SEPTEMBER · OCTOBER

Jewish New Year (Rosh Hashanah)

Monday 30

Tuesday 01

Wednesday 02

Thursday 03

Friday 04

First quarter

Saturday 05

Sunday 06

Map of the Philippine Islands, with twelve marginal vignettes engraved after designs by
Francisco Suarez, with illustrations of life in the Philippine Islands and plans of Guam,
Cavite, Zamboanga and Manila, Manila, 1734

OCTOBER

07 Monday

08 Tuesday

09 Wednesday   Day of Atonement (Yom Kippur)

10 Thursday

11 Friday

12 Saturday

13 Sunday   *Full moon*

The New Pictorial Map of London, produced in London by Geographia Ltd., 1931

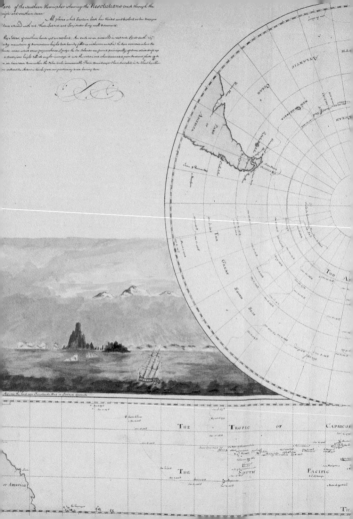

OCTOBER

First day of Tabernacles (Succoth)
Holiday, USA (Columbus Day)
Holiday, Canada (Thanksgiving)

Monday 14

Tuesday 15

Wednesday 16

Thursday 17

Friday 18

Saturday 19

Sunday 20

Detail of a map of the Southern Hemisphere showing the route of the *Resolution* during Captain James Cook's second voyage, from Cape Town in November 1772 to Caledonia in October 1774

OCTOBER

21 Monday   *Last quarter*

_____

22 Tuesday

_____

23 Wednesday

_____

24 Thursday

_____

25 Friday

_____

26 Saturday

_____

27 Sunday   British Summer Time ends

_____

A dissected globe; the segments form eight cross-sections, six of these show maps
of the continents on their upper surfaces and illustrations with text on their lower
surfaces, produced in London by A. & N. Myers, c.1866

Notes

OCTOBER · NOVEMBER

New moon
Holiday, Republic of Ireland
Holiday, New Zealand (Labour Day)

Monday 28

Tuesday 29

Wednesday 30

Halloween

Thursday 31

All Saints' Day

Friday 01

Saturday 02

Sunday 03

A map of the world showing the voyages of Captain James Cook, from *Tallis's Illustrated Atlas, and Modern History of the World, Geographical, Political, Commercial, and Statistical*, published in London by John Tallis and Co., 1851

NOVEMBER

04 Monday   *First quarter*

---

05 Tuesday   Guy Fawkes

---

06 Wednesday

---

07 Thursday

---

08 Friday

---

09 Saturday

---

10 Sunday   Remembrance Sunday

Chart of Palmerston Island, with coastal view. Captain James Cook reached this small
island, near Niue, on 16 June 1774

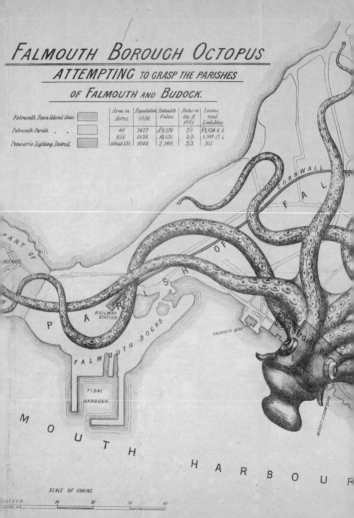

FALMOUTH BOROUGH OCTOPUS

ATTEMPTING TO GRASP THE PARISHES

OF FALMOUTH AND BUDOCK.

	Area in Acres.	Population 1881.	Rateable Value	Rates in the £ 1881	Loans and Liabilities
Falmouth Town Colored thus.	40	3673	£9,070	7/0	£8,039 6 8
Falmouth Parish „	654	6158	19,621	5/8	8,598 13 4
Penwerris Lighting District.	about 151	1046	2,568	3/3	Nil.

CORNWALL

PART OF

PARISH OF FAL

RAILWAY STATION

FALMOUTH DOCKS

FALMOUTH QUAY

TIDAL HARBOUR.

MOUTH HARBOUR

SCALE OF CHAINS.

10   20   30   40

NOVEMBER

Holiday, USA (Veterans Day)
Holiday, Canada (Remembrance Day)

Monday 11

Full moon

Tuesday 12

Wednesday 13

Thursday 14

Friday 15

Saturday 16

Sunday 17

Detail of a political map of Falmouth with an octopus superimposed over a plan
of the area, denoting perceived attempts at expansion by Falmouth borough,
produced in London by Edwin T. Olver, c.1885

NOVEMBER

18 Monday

19 Tuesday   *Last quarter*

20 Wednesday

21 Thursday

22 Friday

23 Saturday

24 Sunday

Detail of a map of South Africa, published in Middelburgh by Barent Langenes, 1598

Mete

Debsan

Zet mon

Terra baixa
G. duos serras
Terratto
Mont Negro montes
Terra baixa
P. breua
G. c as 1 deas
Terradas mesas
C. de Ruypyz
Praya das neues
G. Frio
P. das Pedras

Gunga

Zambre

Carma

Armeto

Bagametro

Luema

Gallila

Armeta

Lacus Sachaf

Bera

Cumar

Dodel

Matac hazi

Agag

Augesa

Beif

Gebage

Bone

Caburas

Butua

Amara

Ghrai

Cefala

Quiticui

Motanea

G. de S. Ambrosio
Orostro da pedia
P. Dostico
Tallo
C. de S. Thome
G. da coceptio
Terra baixa
Medaos

Bafat

Iotama

C. de S. Mari

Zabro

Heuggo

C. de S. Seba

MONO

Garma

Monomotapa

P. S. Maria

MOTAPA

G. santos

Cumssa

Beligaras

S. Li

Praio

Samot

Medaos

Peseria

P. das Ilhos

Vigita

de ouro

P. de S. N

G. das voltas
Ysticos secos montes

maga

Cordada

Terra do N

Pira
Pramu

Osmaros d Pedra
montes

B. de

Alombadas das sarcas

Lagoas

Periado das Fonte

G. de S. Elena
uada de soldanha

C. Falco
C. das Agulhas
C. de Infantz

L. Chaus

Bonæ spei

C. de Aros
B. ffem

NOVEMBER · DECEMBER

Monday 25

New moon

Tuesday 26

Wednesday 27

Holiday, USA (Thanksgiving)

Thursday 28

Friday 29

St Andrew's Day

Saturday 30

First Sunday in Advent

Sunday 01

Comic Map of the British Isles Indicating the Political Situation in 1880, by Frederick W. Rose, published in London by G.W. Bacon & Co., 1880

DECEMBER

02 Monday

03 Tuesday

04 Wednesday   *First quarter*

05 Thursday

06 Friday

07 Saturday

08 Sunday

Detail of a picture-map of Central Tibet in seven sections, 1844–1862

DECEMBER

Monday 09

Tuesday 10

Wednesday 11

Full moon   Thursday 12

Friday 13

Saturday 14

Sunday 15

An Illustrative Map of Human Life, a religious allegory of the human condition from infancy to the grave, drawn and engraved by John Ping, published in London by James Nisbet, 1833

DECEMBER

16 Monday

17 Tuesday

18 Wednesday

19 Thursday   *Last quarter*

20 Friday

21 Saturday

22 Sunday   Winter Solstice (Winter begins)
                                                 Hannukah begins (at sunset)

Detail of a nineteenth-century Chinese coloured map of the town of Amoy (Xiamen)

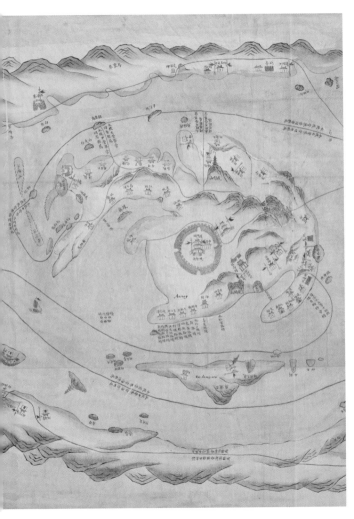

DECEMBER

Monday 23

Christmas Eve

Tuesday 24

Christmas Day
Holiday, UK, Republic of Ireland, USA,
Canada, Australia and New Zealand

Wednesday 25

New moon
Boxing Day (St Stephen's Day)
Holiday, UK, Republic of Ireland, Canada,
Australia and New Zealand

Thursday 26

Friday 27

Saturday 28

Sunday 29

Engraving of a map of the Moon drawn by Jean Dominique Cassini, Paris, c.1679

30 Monday

Hannukah ends

31 Tuesday

New Year's Eve

01 Wednesday

New Year's Day
Holiday, UK, Republic of Ireland, USA, Canada,
Australia and New Zealand

02 Thursday

Holiday, Scotland and New Zealand

03 Friday

04 Saturday

05 Sunday

A pictorial map of European Russia, produced in Warsaw by M.I. Tomasik, 1903

Наглядная карта Европейской Россіи

Условные знаки

YEAR PLANNER

JANUARY	JULY
FEBRUARY	AUGUST
MARCH	SEPTEMBER
APRIL	OCTOBER
MAY	NOVEMBER
JUNE	DECEMBER